Breaking

A Guide to Healing for Adult Children of Emotionally Immature Parents

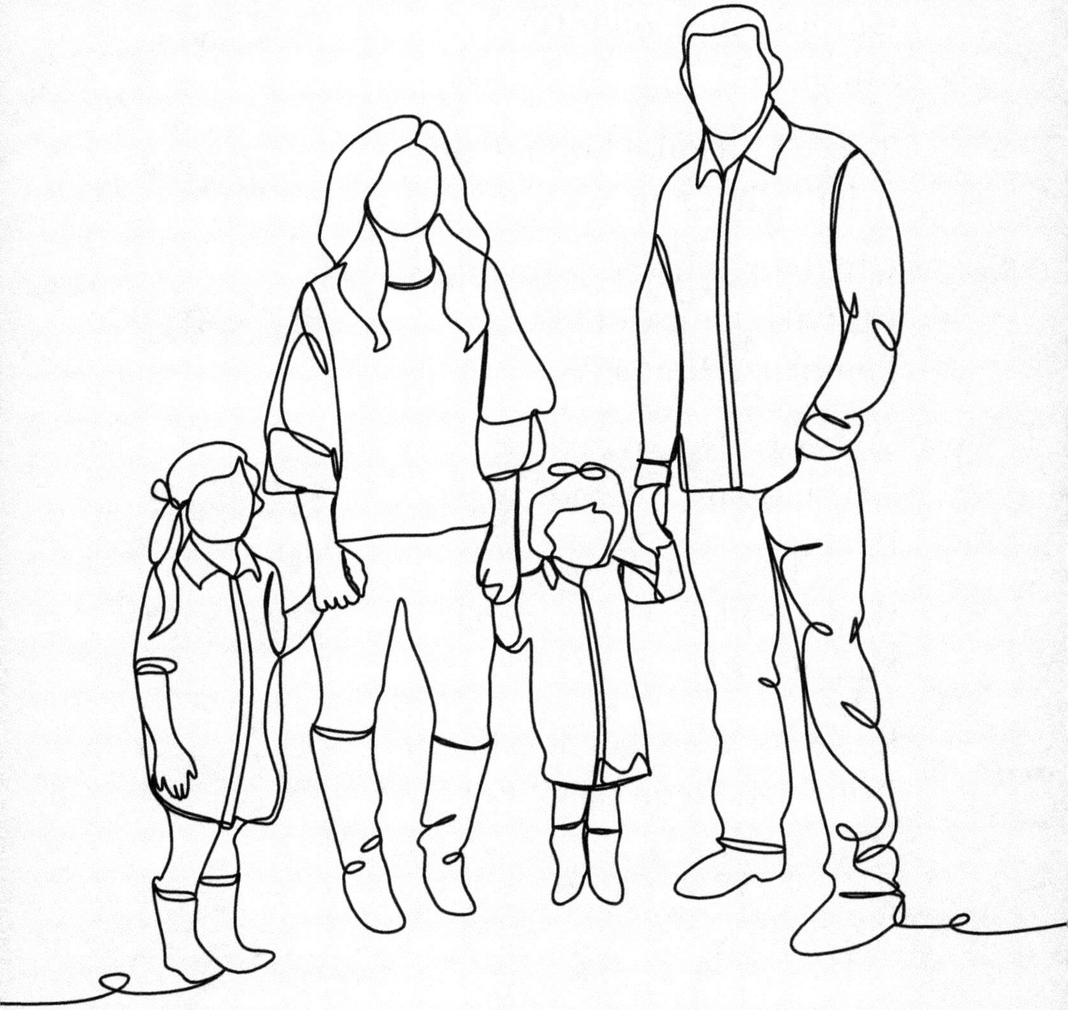

Table of Contents

Introduction — PAGE 1

Understanding Emotionally Immature Parents — PAGE 2

The Emotional Impact on Adult Children — PAGE 13

Children who're growing Up with Emotionally Immature Parents — PAGE 19

Ways to Recover and Heal After Being Raised by EI Parents — PAGE 46

How to Stop Emotionally Immature — PAGE 53

Lessons We Learned From Adult Children of EI Parents — PAGE 65

Introduction

Have you ever felt like you're carrying the weight of your past on your shoulders, a heavy burden that seems to seep into every aspect of your life? Do you find yourself struggling with your emotions, relationships, and self-worth, unable to fully shake off the ghosts of your upbringing? If so, you are not alone.

This book is a guide and a lifeline for those who have navigated the challenging waters of growing up with emotionally immature parents. It is for the sons and daughters who, from a young age, learned to adapt, to cope, and to survive in the shadow of caregivers who may have been distant, rejecting, or self-involved. It's for those who, as adults, carry the scars of their childhood, often hidden beneath a veneer of strength, resilience, and maturity.

Emotionally immature parents can cast a long and profound shadow over their children's lives. Their inability to provide the emotional support, understanding, and guidance that their sons and daughters needed can leave lasting wounds. Yet, there is hope, healing, and transformation waiting for those willing to embark on the journey of self-discovery and recovery.

CHAPTER 1

Understanding Emotionally Immature Parents

Growing up with emotionally immature parents can leave children feeling unseen and unheard. They may also find it difficult to fully express their own emotions.

What is an emotionally immature parent?

Research suggests emotional maturity is one of three key areas of overall maturity important for parenthood.

Emotional maturity allows parents to shift their focus from themselves to how their reactions, behaviors, and emotional expression affect their children.

Emotionally immature parents aren't always able to recognize and acknowledge their children's emotions. According to Dr. Laura Louis, a licensed psychologist from Marietta, Georgia, this can lead to unintentional neglect.

Emotional neglect may contribute to insecure attachment styles in adulthood. Attachment style in psychology theory states your relationships with caregivers during childhood determine how securely, or insecurely, you form attachments in adulthood.

Signs of emotionally immature parents

1. Emotional reactivity

Emotional reactivity is the intensity with which you respond to emotions. High emotional reactivity is a sign of poor emotional regulation and involves intense shifts in your emotional responses.

In parenthood, it can look like extreme emotional reactions to minor inconveniences, quickly shifting from one mood to another, or reacting to emotions without thought.

Examples of high emotional reactivity in parents include:

- extreme emotional outbursts
- throwing tantrums when a child doesn't respond as desired
- threatening or punishing children for displaying emotions
- relying on children for adult emotional support
- being unpredictable in your emotional responses

High emotional reactivity can make children feel unsafe to express emotions.

2. Emotional unavailability

Sometimes emotional immaturity in parents looks like emotional unavailability. This can come through in behaviors that seem aloof, disinterested, or unconcerned with a child's needs.

Chadley Zobolas, a licensed clinical social worker from Denver, Colorado, gives the example of responding to an upset child with "it could be so much worse."

"This response inadvertently tells children that their experiences aren't 'bad enough' to feel emotions about, and/or that their body's natural emotional experience is wrong, selfish, and something to feel shameful about," she says.

Emotionally unavailable parents may also:
- never demonstrate or verbally express affection
- only offer criticism
- avoid offering comfort when a child is upset
- prioritize personal needs
- avoid open communication
- not show support for a child's interests or activities
- lie about their feelings

Emotionally immature parents who are unavailable emotionally can leave children feeling insecure, anxious, and unable to express themselves emotionally.

3. Lack of empathy

Overall, many of the characteristics seen in emotional immaturity are related to a lack of empathy. Empathy is your ability to relate to the experiences, emotions, and thoughts of other people.
When you can't connect through a shared interpersonal experience, you're unable to recognize how your emotions impact those around you.
Lack of empathy can influence emotional reactivity and emotional withdrawal. It can also contribute to behaviors of emotionally immature parents, such as:
- defensiveness
- complaining
- personal boundary-crossing
- stonewalling
- ignoring
- insensitive comments
- blame-shifting

- interrupting
- inattentiveness
- making impulsive decisions that involve children without regard to their wants or needs

Types Of Emotionally Immature Parents

1. Emotional Parents

Like their name indicates, they are run by their feelings. Their feelings drive their actions and behaviors. They might be overwhelming and then abruptly withdraw from you. They need others - you - to stabilize their feelings. Small slights of the world are treated like catastrophic moments. You feel this.

You are either a rescuer or abandoner. Their instability and unpredictability make for a very dynamic and chaotic upbringing because you never know what to expect. They are overwhelmed by anxiety, and you too become riddled by their anxiety and can also become anxious. You never know what to expect.

As they are emotionally falling apart, they are taking you with them. You will experience all their hatred, rage, disappointment, and despair. You feel like you are walking on eggshells. Hint: you are. They have a difficult time tolerating any type of stress. They see life in black and white, holding onto grudges, and use emotional tactics to control you.

Signs of an emotional parent: (among others)
- Preoccupied with his or her own needs.
- Has low empathy.
- Communication is not reciprocal, but focused on them.
- Has poor relationship repair skills.
- Is reactive, not thoughtful, or self-reflective.

2. Driven Parents.

At first glance, driven parents might appear to be normal. They are getting things done. However, if you were raised by driven parents the irony is you might end up being unmotivated or lacking in self-control. This is because a driven' parent's mindset is that you have the same goals and approach to life as they do.
They know what's good for you. They have the answers. They don't encourage separate paths or goals for you but selectively give praise for what they want to see and push away the rest.
Your parents upbringing was also not emotionally available and in an **emotionally deprived environment**. They got by going it alone. They are self-made and proud of their independence and have raised you the same way. They continue this unhealthy legacy issue.
You might feel constantly evaluated for how much and what you are doing. They might also coddle you in a way because they feel you cannot do anything right. They were not attuned to your needs but focused on what they felt you should be doing. It's never ending.

Goal oriented and super busy they seek to perfect everything around them, including you and others. They seek to control and interfere with your life. Because they are so driven, they seldom take the time to hit the pause button and provide empathy and comfort to you.

Signs of a driven parent: (among others)
- Has low empathy.
- Preoccupied with his or her own needs.
- Is reactive and not thoughtful.
- Likes to run the show.
- Sees him or herself as a fixer.

3. Passive Parents.

They take a 'hands off' and laissez-faire approach to dealing with whatever life throws at them. Although comparatively they are less harmful than the other types, this type of parenting still has negative effects. They may allow abuse or neglect by the parent towards you by turning their cheek and ignoring it, and looking the other way. This makes you feel like they are too abusing you but in a different way. They are emotionally neglecting you. They minimize and acquiesce to problems.
They tend to have partners who are more intense but equally emotionally immature. When life becomes challenging or intense, they check out and withdraw. They are more likely to be like an ostrich - stick their head in the sand. They are equally immature and self-absorbed and self-involved as the other types but can often get away with this type of parenting because they come across as being more playful.

They show more empathy - but only if you are not getting in the way of their needs. Because they stick their head in the sand or turn a blind eye, you feel like your parent isn't available to or for you. You might also grow up to feel truly helpless and passive in their own life's direction and path.

Signs of a passive parent: (among others)
- Is preoccupied with his or her needs.
- Has little empathy.
- Is either too close and enmeshed or too distant.
- Can be fun, but not protective.
- Can be at times, emotionally intimate.

4. Rejecting Parents.

They are walled off and prefer to spend time alone. You get the feeling early on that your parent would rather not be around you. You are a bother. Your parent gets annoyed when you ask for something. The child learns not to approach their parent. If you are seeking compassion, understanding, or affection, your parent may become angry at you. They look at you like you are a bother. It's a terrible feeling.
They have a hands-off approach to you feel bothered by their presence. They don't enjoy emotional intimacy. You will find them blowing up, demanding or commanding, and isolating from family life. You might wonder why they even have children - why did they have you if they don't want you around? They prefer to be left alone and do their own thing. They rule the home, and you know and feel that.

You walk on eggshells so as not to upset or bother them. You come to see yourself as a bother to others or irritating so they will give up easily.
Signs of a rejecting parent: (among others)
- Is preoccupied with his or her needs.
- Has little empathy.
- Likes to mock and dismiss.
- Is often rejecting and angry.
- Isn't self-reflective.

Identify the "Red Flags" of EI Parents

Lack of empathy

While emotionally immature parents are very capable of emotional outbursts to release internal pressure, they find it difficult to put themselves in the child's shoes. Understanding what is going on from another person's perspective and how the child must feel is challenging for them. They also find it hard to open up, and share how vulnerable they feel, so it's no wonder this gap prevents the creation of deep, tender and trusting relationships.

Inconsistent or unpredictable behaviour patterns

Dealing with parental mood swings often leaves children confused, unsettled, and insecure. Children never really know what to expect; they lack a sense of stability because what was ok one day is not ok the next. They feel loved and accepted one day and get shamed and pushed away the next.

Likewise, it's a guessing game to anticipate the parents' response. Will they lose their cool for something trivial and then dismiss an important incident? This profoundly impacts the child. The inconsistency and unpredictability can make children feel on edge and challenge the development of a stable sense of self.

Difficulties in taking responsibility

Most of us find it challenging to admit mistakes and to apologise. EI Parents tend to struggle to take responsibility for things they did wrong or acknowledge their behaviour's impact on their children. They often deflect blame or find excuses. As this is modelled, it is not surprising for the children to adopt the role of a victim. This makes it hard for children not to take responsibility.

Having unclear boundaries

In regression sessions, clients often share how heavy they felt when mum or dad shared their own burdens with them. It felt too much; they struggled because they felt the need to lift that burden - they tried and failed. Imagine the stress for the little one.. Another sign of lacking boundaries is the constant need to know everything in the child's life.

You may have experienced it when one of your parents went through your personal belongings, read your diary, or listened in on a conversation you had with your best friend.This often continues, even when the "little one" is already in their 40s. Then they become upset when suddenly nothing gets shared with them anymore.

Emotionally immature parents may struggle to acknowledge and respect their child's thoughts, feelings, and choices. They may dismiss or invalidate their child's perspectives, impose their own beliefs and desires onto them, or fail to recognize their child as a separate individual with their own autonomy.

CHAPTER 2

The Emotional Impact on Adult Children

Emotions play a vital role in our development, shaping our personality, and influencing our decisions. Children's emotions can have a significant impact on their future development and adult life. Emotional development begins in infancy, and it is influenced by a wide range of factors, including genetics, environmental factors, and parental behaviour.

Discussion

It is significant to highlight that during infancy, children develop emotional bonds with their caregivers, which are critical for emotional development. These bonds provide a sense of security, which allows children to explore the world around them confidently. As children grow older, they begin to develop a more complex emotional repertoire, including a range of emotions such as joy, sadness, anger, and fear. Several factors can influence a child's emotional development, including genetics, environment, and parental behaviour. Research has shown that children's emotional development is partially determined by their genetics. Studies have found that 'children with parents who have anxiety or depression are more likely to experience emotional problems', suggesting that genes play a role in emotional development.

The environment also plays a significant role in emotional development. Children who grow up in unstable or unsafe environments are more likely to experience emotional problems such as anxiety and depression. Adverse childhood experiences such as abuse, neglect, and exposure to violence can have long-lasting effects on a child's emotional development, leading to problems in adulthood. It should be also emphasised that parental behaviour determines emotional development of humans. Parents who are warm, supportive, and responsive to their children's emotional needs are more likely to have children with healthy emotional development.

It can be assumed that emotional problems that develop in childhood can persist into adulthood, affecting a person's mental health and quality of life. For example, 'children who experience anxiety or depression are more likely to have mental health problems in adulthood, including anxiety disorders and depression. Consequently, emotions experienced in childhood may lead also to posttraumatic disorders. While PTSD is commonly associated with experiences such as combat, accidents, or natural disasters, it is important to recognize that childhood emotions and experiences can also contribute to the development of PTSD. Children who undergo traumatic events or highly distressing emotional experiences, such as abuse, neglect, violence, or the loss of a loved one, are at risk of developing PTSD. These events can overwhelm a child's ability to cope and lead to persistent and disruptive symptoms that affect their emotional well-being.

It is important to note that not all individuals who experience childhood trauma will develop posttraumatic stress disorder (PTSD). Factors such as the severity of the event, the availability of support systems, and individual resilience play a role in determining the likelihood of PTSD development'. Additionally, 'the presence of other risk factors, such as a history of previous trauma, genetic predisposition, or a lack of supportive relationships, can increase the vulnerability to developing PTSD'.

Emotional problems in childhood can also affect one's social and interpersonal relationships in adulthood.

Children who have difficulty regulating their emotions may struggle to form positive relationships with others, leading to loneliness and social isolation in adulthood. In contrast, children who have healthy emotional development are more likely to form positive relationships and have fulfilling social lives in adulthood. Similarly, adults who were raised in a supportive and nurturing environment tend to have better emotional regulation and coping skills, higher levels of resilience, and stronger social support networks. Emotional development in childhood can also influence a person's career and academic success in adulthood. Children who have healthy emotional development are more likely to have higher self-esteem, be more resilient, and have effective coping mechanisms. These skills are essential for success in the workplace and academic settings. Therefore, adults who have difficulty managing their emotions may also experience relationship problems, work-related stress, and physical health problems. For example, chronic stress can lead to a weakened immune system, increased blood pressure, and a higher risk of heart disease.

Despite the long-term impact of childhood emotions, adults can still learn to manage their emotions and improve their mental health and well-being. Some effective strategies for managing emotions include:

1. Mindfulness meditation: Mindfulness meditation involves paying attention to the present moment without judgment. This practice has been shown to improve emotional regulation and reduce symptoms of anxiety and depression

2. Cognitive-behavioral therapy: Cognitive-behavioral therapy is a type of therapy that helps individuals identify and change negative thought patterns and behaviors. This therapy has been shown to be effective for treating a range of mental health problems, including anxiety and depression

3. Exercise: Regular exercise has been shown to reduce symptoms of anxiety and depression and improve overall mental health and well-being

4. Social support: Building strong social support networks can help individuals manage stress and improve their mental health

Conclusion

In conclusion, the emotional development of children has a profound impact on their adult lives. Emotional bonds formed during infancy with caregivers provide a foundation for secure exploration and the development of a complex emotional repertoire. Genetics, environment, and parental behavior are significant factors influencing emotional development. Research suggests that children of parents with anxiety or depression are more likely to experience emotional problems, highlighting the role of genetics. The environment, particularly adverse childhood experiences, can have long-lasting effects on emotional development.

Parental behavior plays a crucial role in emotional development, with warm and supportive parents fostering healthy emotional development, while cold and unresponsive parents may contribute to emotional problems. Emotional difficulties that arise in childhood often persist into adulthood, affecting mental health and overall quality of life. These challenges can impact social relationships, leading to loneliness and social isolation, or positive emotional development, facilitating fulfilling relationships and strong social support networks.

Moreover, emotional development in childhood can influence an individual's career and academic success. Those with healthy emotional development tend to have higher self-esteem, resilience, and effective coping mechanisms, essential for success in various settings. Difficulties in managing emotions can lead to relationship problems, work-related stress, and physical health issues. Fortunately, adults can still learn to manage their emotions and improve their mental well-being. Strategies such as mindfulness meditation, cognitive-behavioral therapy, regular exercise, and building social support networks have shown effectiveness in enhancing emotional regulation, reducing anxiety and depression symptoms, and improving overall mental health.

Understanding the significance of emotional development in childhood enables individuals to address emotional challenges and work towards achieving healthier emotional well-being. By investing in emotional regulation and seeking support, individuals can positively impact their mental health, relationships, and overall life satisfaction.

CHAPTER 3

Children who're growing Up with Emotionally Immature Parents

Growing up with emotionally immature parents can be challenging and happens in many homes. These parents, often unintentionally, leave an indelible mark on their offspring's emotional landscapes, with lasting consequences.

When you have lived with an emotionally immature, unavailable, or inordinately self-centered parent, you may still feel anger, loneliness, betrayal, and abandonment might linger in you.

You'll need to develop emotional maturity and practical insights into your feelings of anger and loneliness to heal. When your emotional needs aren't met, discover ways to be more present to your feelings and emotional needs. Allow for honest insight into your pain. Stay connected to yourself without zoning out or dulling yourself.

Possible patterns developed when growing up:
- With neglectful parents, you may neglect your own emotions or self-care.

- With a driven parent who doesn't make time for their children, you may seek to prove yourself worthy of love through an obsession with work or overgiving to others.

- With immature, unavailable, or selfish parents, you may be inaccessible to your friends, partner, or children. Or you may protect yourself with defenses; being vulnerable and open can feel too threatening.

- With a reactive or emotional parent, you might avoid conflict and stuff your needs or emotions, caretaking to the people in your life.

- With a rejecting parent, you may reject yourself and deny your own needs to keep others happy.

- With difficult or autocratic parents where there is little consideration for your perspective or feelings, you may not be in touch with your needs or feel paralyzed when making decisions because you never got practice growing up.

However, no matter what kind of childhood you experienced, you can connect with the compass of your true self, learning the genuine nature of relationships beginning with yourself.

"Breaking the Cycle of Emotional Immaturity"

In a quiet suburban neighborhood, there lived a family with two children, Sarah and Michael. Their parents, Emily and Daniel, were emotionally immature, and their home was often filled with turmoil.

Emily had difficulty expressing her emotions and frequently acted out her frustrations with passive-aggressive behavior. She rarely acknowledged her children's feelings and needs, leaving Sarah and Michael feeling unheard and unimportant. On the other hand, Daniel was self-centered, often prioritizing his own desires over the well-being of his family. He struggled to empathize with his children's struggles and rarely offered them emotional support.

As Sarah and Michael grew older, they began to recognize the impact of their parents' emotional immaturity on their own lives. Sarah, the older sibling, developed low self-esteem and was a perfectionist, always seeking validation from others. She struggled with forming healthy relationships, often being overly dependent on her friends for emotional support.

Michael, the younger of the two, became withdrawn and emotionally guarded. He had trouble expressing his feelings and tended to keep them bottled up inside. His lack of emotional connection with others made it challenging for him to build meaningful relationships, both with friends and potential romantic partners.

Despite the challenges they faced, Sarah and Michael were determined not to perpetuate the cycle of emotional immaturity in their own lives. They knew that breaking free from this cycle was essential for their future happiness and the well-being of their own families.

They began seeking help through therapy, reading self-help books, and attending support groups. Sarah worked on her self-esteem and learned to set healthy boundaries in her relationships. Michael started opening up to trusted friends and slowly learned to express his emotions in a healthy way.

Over time, their parents, Emily and Daniel, started noticing the positive changes in their children. Emily began to recognize her own emotional shortcomings and started seeking therapy to work on her communication skills and emotional awareness. Daniel, too, started to realize the importance of empathy and support for his children.

As the years passed, Sarah and Michael grew into emotionally mature adults. They each built strong, supportive relationships and families of their own. They made sure to provide their children with the emotional support and understanding they had longed for in their own childhoods.

Their journey from growing up with emotionally immature parents to becoming emotionally healthy adults was not easy, but it was worth it. Sarah and Michael had broken the cycle, creating a brighter and more emotionally fulfilling future for themselves and the generations to come.

The story of Sarah and Michael serves as a reminder that with determination, self-awareness, and the right support, one can break free from the constraints of an emotionally immature upbringing and build a healthier, happier life.

"Breaking the Cycle of Emotional Immaturity" explores the impact of emotionally immature parents on their children, portraying the struggle and emotional wounds that can result. Through the characters of Sarah and Michael, the story highlights the importance of self-awareness, resilience, and personal growth in overcoming these challenges. It also offers a message of hope by illustrating that with determination, therapy, and self-improvement, individuals can break free from such patterns. Additionally, the story emphasizes the potential for transformation in emotionally immature parents, suggesting that awareness can lead to positive change. Ultimately, it conveys the generational impact of emotional growth and the possibility of a brighter future for those who face similar circumstances.

1. "Growing up in a family with emotionally immature parents is a lonely experience."

Lily's Story

Growing up in a family with emotionally immature parents is a lonely experience. For Lily, a young girl with dreams as vast as the sky, this loneliness was a constant companion. Her parents, John and Emma, were good people at heart but struggled to express their emotions. They rarely spoke openly about their feelings, leaving Lily to navigate her emotions alone. In their home, laughter was scarce, and hugs even scarcer.

As Lily ventured into adolescence, the isolation grew heavier. She longed for her parents' understanding and support, especially when facing the complexities of teenage life. But their emotional distance made her feel like an outsider in her own family.

One day, while wandering in a nearby park, Lily met an elderly woman named Eleanor. They struck up a conversation, and as Lily shared her story, Eleanor listened with empathy and kindness. She, too, had experienced the loneliness of growing up with emotionally distant parents. Eleanor became Lily's confidante, offering guidance, encouragement, and a listening ear whenever needed. She taught Lily the value of self-expression and the importance of finding a support system beyond her family.

As Lily continued to confide in Eleanor, she began to discover her own inner strength. She pursued her passions, made close friends who became like a second family, and excelled in school. With Eleanor's wisdom, Lily found her voice and started communicating her needs to her parents, encouraging them to open up emotionally. Over time, John and Emma, inspired by their daughter's courage, began to take steps to improve their emotional awareness. They attended therapy sessions to work on their communication skills and understanding of their own emotions.

The family's journey was challenging, filled with moments of frustration and tears, but also moments of growth and understanding. Gradually, the emotional distance between them began to narrow, and they learned to connect on a deeper level.

As Lily transitioned into adulthood, she carried with her the lessons learned from Eleanor and her family's transformation.

Years later, Lily started a support group for young people facing similar challenges, offering them a safe space to share their experiences and find the support they needed. She believed that no one should have to navigate the loneliness of emotional immaturity alone, and she was determined to make a difference.

In the end, Lily's journey from loneliness to connection not only transformed her life but also touched the lives of others, proving that even in the darkest of circumstances, there is always hope for healing and growth.

"Lily's story" portrays the theme of emotional isolation caused by growing up with emotionally immature parents. It highlights the transformative journey of the protagonist, Lily, who evolves from a lonely child into a resilient and empathetic young adult. The story underscores the importance of external support and mentorship, personified by Eleanor, in coping with such challenges. It emphasizes the significance of open communication and the potential for healing within family relationships. Above all, it conveys a message of hope, illustrating that even in emotionally challenging circumstances, individuals can find empowerment, foster personal growth, and make a positive impact on their lives and the lives of others.

2. "If your parent was scared of deep feelings, you might have felt shame for needing comfort"

Mia's story

In a quiet suburban neighborhood, there lived a young girl named Mia. She had grown up in a home where her mother, Sarah, was scared of deep emotions. Sarah always encouraged Mia to be strong, independent, and never show vulnerability. As a result, Mia often felt shame for needing comfort or expressing her feelings.

One rainy afternoon, Mia's teacher, Ms. Thompson, noticed that Mia seemed unusually quiet and withdrawn. During recess, Ms. Thompson approached Mia and gently asked if everything was okay. Tears welled up in Mia's eyes, and she confessed, "I miss my old stuffed bear, Mr. Cuddles. Mom says I'm too old for it, and I should be strong."

Ms. Thompson, with empathy in her eyes, reassured Mia that it was perfectly okay to have feelings and need comfort. She shared a story about her own childhood teddy bear, Mr. Snuggles, and how he had brought her comfort during tough times. Mia's eyes widened with surprise, realizing that even adults had cherished comfort items.

Inspired by Ms. Thompson's story, Mia decided to confide in her grandmother, Lily, that evening. Lily had always been a warm and loving presence in Mia's life. With tears streaming down her cheeks, Mia admitted her feelings of shame for needing comfort. Lily held Mia close, assuring her that emotions were natural, and seeking comfort was nothing to be ashamed of.

Lily then shared a family secret with Mia: her own mother, Mia's great-grandmother, had struggled with emotional vulnerability due to the hardships she had faced in her youth. This revelation helped Mia understand that her mother, Sarah, had learned her emotional tendencies from her own upbringing.

With Lily's guidance, Mia and Sarah started a journey of healing and understanding. They attended therapy sessions together, learning how to communicate their emotions and support each other. Sarah began to recognize the importance of allowing Mia to express her feelings without judgment.

Over time, their home transformed into a more emotionally nurturing environment. Mia felt safe to express her emotions, and Sarah learned to embrace her own vulnerabilities. Their bond grew stronger as they navigated this emotional journey together.

As Mia blossomed into a confident and emotionally aware young woman, she never forgot the lessons she had learned. She realized that the shame she had once felt for needing comfort was a result of generational patterns, and breaking those patterns had been a powerful transformation.

Mia grew up to become a therapist specializing in helping families break free from the cycle of emotional immaturity. Her own experience of unraveling the threads of shame became a source of strength, inspiring her to empower others to embrace their emotions and seek comfort when needed.

In the end, Mia's story serves as a reminder that the shame children may feel for needing comfort from emotionally immature parents can be transcended with understanding, communication, and the willingness to break free from generational patterns of emotional avoidance.

This story explores the consequences of emotionally immature parents, focusing on Mia's shame for needing comfort due to her mother's emotional limitations. The story emphasizes the importance of empathetic figures, like Ms. Thompson and Mia's grandmother, in helping children navigate such challenges. It underscores the inter-generational nature of emotional behavior, suggesting that patterns can be passed down through families. The story highlights the transformative power of therapy and open communication within families, leading to healing and understanding. Mia's personal growth reflects the theme of empowerment and the ability to break free from generational patterns. Overall, the narrative conveys a message of hope, resilience, and the potential for positive change in the face of emotional immaturity.

3. "Emotional intimacy is profoundly fulfilling, creating a sense of being seen for who you really are."

Ethan's Story

In a tranquil neighborhood, a boy named Ethan grew up in a home with emotionally immature parents, Rachel and James. Their household was often enveloped in silence, with feelings left unspoken.

As he matured, Ethan yearned for something more profound—an emotional intimacy that would make him feel truly seen for who he was.

One sunny afternoon, as Ethan sat alone in the park, he struck up a conversation with an elderly gentleman named Mr. Wallace. They talked about life, dreams, and the beauty of genuine connections. Ethan shared his longing for emotional intimacy, and Mr. Wallace recounted stories of his own past, where heartfelt connections had transformed his life.

Inspired by Mr. Wallace's wisdom, Ethan decided to broach the subject with his parents. One evening, he gently expressed his desire for a deeper emotional connection, confessing that their distant behavior had left him feeling invisible. Rachel and James were taken aback but recognized the truth in his words.

The couple decided to embark on a journey of self-discovery and emotional growth. They sought therapy to address their emotional immaturity, working to understand the root causes of their struggles. It was a challenging process, but they were committed to healing for the sake of their son.

As therapy progressed, Rachel and James began to unveil the layers of their emotional past. They shared their own experiences of feeling unseen and unimportant during their childhoods. These revelations helped them comprehend the profound importance of emotional intimacy in their lives.

Gradually, the family dynamics started to shift. Rachel and James began to communicate their emotions more openly, allowing Ethan to witness their vulnerability. They also encouraged him to share his feelings, creating a safe space for authentic conversations.

In time, Ethan felt the blossoming of emotional intimacy within his family. The heartfelt connections that had eluded them for so long finally started to take root. He felt genuinely seen and heard, and the void that had once filled his heart began to dissipate.

As Ethan grew into a confident and emotionally aware young man, he carried the legacy of emotional intimacy with him. He formed deep, meaningful relationships, cherishing the sense of being seen for who he truly was. The story of Ethan and his family serves as a testament to the transformative power of emotional intimacy. It illustrates that even in emotionally challenging circumstances, individuals and families can embark on a path of healing, growth, and authentic connections. Emotional intimacy, as they discovered, is the portrait of heartfelt connection that enriches lives beyond measure.

4. "The most primitive parts of our brain tell us that safety lies in familiarity."

Emily's Story

Emily grew up in a family where familiarity was the cornerstone of her existence. Her parents, Sarah and John, were emotionally immature and struggled to express their emotions openly.

Their home was a place of routine, where emotional connections were seldom formed.

As a child, Emily found solace in the predictable rhythms of her life. She knew what to expect each day, and this consistency provided a semblance of safety in a world where emotions were often tumultuous.

But as Emily entered her teenage years, a restlessness stirred within her. She yearned for something more, something beyond the familiar routines and emotional detachment that had defined her family life. She began to notice how her friends' families embraced the richness of emotional connections, and she longed to experience the same.

One summer, Emily met a girl named Maya at a local summer camp. Maya's family was known for their warm and open-hearted gatherings. The contrast between Emily's own home life and the welcoming atmosphere at Maya's house was stark, and it left a deep impression on her.

Emily and Maya quickly became close friends, and Emily often found herself spending weekends at Maya's home. There, she experienced the vibrant tapestry of emotions that a loving family could offer. She marveled at how they openly shared their joys and sorrows, creating bonds that felt unbreakable.

Inevitably, Emily began to yearn for a similar emotional richness in her own family. She decided to have a heart-to-heart conversation with her parents, Sarah and John. She expressed her desire for a more emotionally connected family life, even though it meant stepping into unfamiliar territory.

She expressed her desire for a more emotionally connected family life, even though it meant stepping into unfamiliar territory.

At first, her parents were resistant to change, as the most primitive parts of their brains told them that safety lay in familiarity. However, witnessing Emily's determination and recognizing their own shortcomings, they decided to seek therapy to address their emotional immaturity.

Therapy opened a door to emotional growth for Sarah and John. They confronted their fear of change and embraced the idea of creating a more emotionally connected family environment. It was a challenging process, but they were committed to providing Emily with the sense of safety and emotional richness she longed for.

Over time, the family's started to express their emotions more openly, creating a space for genuine connections to flourish. Emily watched as her parents transformed into emotionally aware individuals, and her heart swelled with gratitude.

As she entered adulthood, Emily carried with her the lessons learned from her journey.

She understood that while the most primitive parts of our brain might seek safety in familiarity, true growth and fulfillment often lie in embracing the unfamiliar and challenging the status quo.

Emily's story serves as a testament to the transformative power of embracing change and emotional growth. It illustrates that even in families with emotionally immature parents, it is possible to break free from the safety of familiarity and find safety in the warmth of emotional connections.

5. "Adults who were emotionally neglected as children can't believe anyone would accept them as they are. So they play a role that puts others first."

Alex's Story

Alex grew up in a household where emotional needs were often ignored. His parents, Mark and Lisa, were emotionally immature, struggling to connect with their own feelings, let alone those of their children. As a result, Alex learned to put others first from a young age, believing that his own needs and emotions didn't matter.

As Alex entered adulthood, the echoes of his emotionally neglected childhood continued to resonate in his life. He had trouble believing that anyone would truly accept him for who he was, complete with his flaws and vulnerabilities. Instead, he wore a mask, playing the role of the selfless, accommodating friend who always put others' needs before his own.

One day, Alex crossed paths with Sarah, a vibrant and perceptive woman who saw through his facade. She recognized the burden he carried and the emotional walls he had built around himself. Determined to help him break free, she offered a genuine friendship that allowed him to slowly lower his guard.

Over time, Sarah encouraged Alex to open up about his past and the emotional neglect he had experienced as a child. She listened without judgment, offering a safe space for him to share his deepest wounds and fears. Her acceptance and understanding began to chip away at the belief that no one would accept him as he truly was.

As Alex started to confront his past and the role he had played for so long, he decided to seek therapy. Through therapy, he learned to recognize the impact of emotional neglect on his self-worth and his tendency to put others' needs before his own. He worked on building self-compassion and self-acceptance, realizing that he deserved love and acceptance just as much as anyone else.

Sarah remained a steadfast friend throughout Alex's journey, supporting him as he navigated the unfamiliar terrain of self-acceptance. She showed him that he didn't need to play a role to be valued and loved. Slowly, he began to shed the mask he had worn for so many years, revealing his authentic self to those around him.

As Alex continued to grow emotionally, he discovered that he could be both caring and authentic. He learned that true friends accepted him for who he was, flaws and all. This newfound sense of self-acceptance allowed him to build deeper, more meaningful relationships, not by putting others first, but by being his genuine self.

The story of Alex is a testament to the power of acceptance and understanding in breaking free from the cycle of emotional neglect. It shows that even adults who were emotionally neglected as children can learn to embrace their true selves and find acceptance among those who value them for who they are, not for the roles they play.

6. "Emotionally immature parents don't know how to validate their child's feelings and instincts. Without this validation, children learn to give in to what others seem sure about."

Peter's Story

In a quiet suburban neighborhood, there lived a boy named Peter, who grew up in a home with emotionally immature parents, Daniel and Maria. Their inability to validate his feelings and instincts left Peter feeling unsure of himself and constantly seeking validation from others.

As a child, Peter often found himself questioning his own judgments and decisions. His parents rarely acknowledged his feelings or offered guidance, which led him to doubt his own intuition. This lack of validation left him feeling lost and dependent on others for assurance.

One day, while Peter was exploring the woods near his house, he met an elderly woman named Mrs. Walker. She had a calming presence and a keen understanding of the human psyche. Peter opened up to her about his struggles with self-doubt and his constant need for validation.

Mrs. Walker listened empathetically and shared stories from her own life. She explained that emotional immaturity often stemmed from her own parents' struggles and their inability to validate her feelings. She told Peter that self-validation was a journey he could embark on, no matter where he started.

Inspired by Mrs. Walker's wisdom, Peter decided to start his journey toward self-validation. He began keeping a journal, where he recorded his thoughts, feelings, and decisions. Through journaling, he learned to recognize his own emotions and instincts, gradually gaining confidence in his ability to trust himself.

Peter also joined a support group for young adults with similar experiences. The group provided a safe space for sharing stories and strategies for self-validation. It was there that Peter realized he wasn't alone in his struggles, and he gained valuable insights from others on his journey.

As Peter continued to explore his emotions and instincts, he faced challenges along the way. There were times when he faltered and sought validation from others out of habit. However, with practice and perseverance, he learned to pause, reflect, and trust his own judgment.

Over time, Peter's newfound self-validation transformed his life. He became more confident in his decisions, trusted his instincts, and developed a strong sense of self-worth. His relationships with others also improved, as he no longer relied on them for constant validation.

As he reached adulthood, Peter continued to carry the lessons learned from his journey. He understood that emotionally immature parents, like his own, might not know how to validate their child's feelings and instincts. However, he knew that he could break free from this cycle and provide validation for himself and others.

The story of Peter serves as a testament to the power of self-validation and personal growth. It illustrates that even in the face of emotional immaturity, individuals can learn to trust their feelings and instincts, freeing themselves from the need for external validation and building a stronger sense of self.

7. "Mutual emotional responsiveness is the single most important ingredient of human relationships."

Mary's Story

In a quaint suburban neighborhood, Marry grew up in a family where emotional intimacy was scarce. Her parents, David and Julia, were emotionally immature, often struggling to communicate their own feelings, let alone respond to Marry's emotions. This left Marry yearning for a deeper connection based on mutual emotional responsiveness.

As Marry entered her teenage years, she became increasingly aware of the emotional void in her family. She craved a sense of understanding and connection that had been missing for so long. Her quest for mutual emotional responsiveness led her to an unexpected encounter with Mr. Wilson, a wise and empathetic neighbor.

Mr. Wilson had experienced his own share of emotional challenges in the past and could relate to Marry's longing for a more emotionally connected family. He shared stories of his own journey towards mutual emotional responsiveness and emphasized its importance in nurturing healthy relationships.

Inspired by Mr. Wilson's wisdom, Marry decided to address the issue with her parents. She courageously opened up to David and Julia, expressing her desire for a deeper emotional connection within the family. She explained how their emotional immaturity had affected her and how she yearned for their understanding and responsiveness.

David and Julia, though initially surprised, recognized the truth in Marry's words. They realized that their emotional limitations had impacted their daughter deeply. They decided to seek therapy as a family, with the goal of learning how to communicate their emotions and become more responsive to each other's needs.
Therapy became a transformative journey for Marry, David, and Julia. They confronted their emotional baggage and learned to express their feelings openly.

They practiced active listening, empathy, and validation, creating a safe space for authentic and responsive conversations.

Over time, their family dynamic began to shift. They started to respond to each other's emotions with understanding and care. Marry no longer felt isolated and unseen but instead found solace in the mutual emotional responsiveness that was slowly becoming a cornerstone of their family life.

As Marry reached adulthood, she carried the lessons learned from her journey into her own relationships. She understood that mutual emotional responsiveness was indeed the single most important ingredient of human relationships. She made it a point to prioritize emotional connection and responsiveness in her interactions, forging meaningful and fulfilling connections with friends, partners, and colleagues.

Marry's story serves as a testament to the transformative power of mutual emotional responsiveness. It illustrates that even in families with emotionally immature parents, individuals can learn to understand, validate, and respond to each other's emotions, ultimately fostering deeper and more meaningful relationships based on trust, empathy, and connection.

8. "Children of immature parents try to help their parents by being low maintenance and appearing not to have any needs."

Taylor's Story

In a picturesque town, Taylor grew up in a household where emotional expression was a foreign language. Susan and Michael, Taylor's parents, were emotionally immature, often drowning in their own unresolved conflicts. To shield their parents from further distress, Taylor became a master at suppressing their own needs and desires, appearing low maintenance on the surface.

As Taylor entered adolescence, the silent sacrifices began to take a toll. The weight of unspoken emotions and unmet needs bore heavy on their heart. One day, while strolling through the town's park, Taylor encountered Clara, an elderly woman with a sparkling aura of wisdom and empathy.

Clara noticed the sadness in Taylor's eyes and struck up a conversation. Taylor, usually guarded, felt an instant connection and opened up about their silent sacrifices. Clara, having weathered her own storms in the past, could relate to the longing for emotional connection. She shared stories of her journey toward self-discovery and emotional healing.

Inspired by Clara's wisdom and warmth, Taylor decided to embark on a path of self-discovery. They sought solace in a journal, where they poured their thoughts and emotions onto the pages. This act of self-expression gradually helped Taylor unearth their buried desires and feelings.

Over time, Taylor's journey toward self-expression and healing became a beacon of hope. They felt the growing urge to confront their parents and initiate a transformation within their family. With newfound courage, Taylor initiated an open-hearted conversation with Susan and Michael.

In a touching exchange, Taylor expressed their longing for emotional connection and revealed the silent sacrifices they had made for the family's sake. Susan and Michael, taken aback yet enlightened by their child's vulnerability, decided to seek therapy as a family.

Therapy became a transformative voyage for Taylor, Susan, and Michael. They learned to communicate their emotions openly, practicing empathy and understanding. The family's bonds strengthened as they journeyed together toward emotional maturity.

As Taylor matured into adulthood, they carried the lessons learned from their journey. They understood that silent sacrifices were a survival mechanism in a family with emotionally immature parents. Taylor had dared to break free from the cycle, embracing self-expression and initiating open communication, ultimately fostering healthier family dynamics.

The story of Taylor resonates as a testament to the human spirit's resilience and capacity for healing. It illustrates the power of self-expression, the significance of seeking support from others who understand our struggles, and the transformative potential of open communication within families.

Taylor's journey is a beautiful symphony of self-discovery, emotional growth, and the courage to unveil the heart's song.

9. "Adult success doesn't completely erase the effects of parental disconnection in childhood."

Elen's Story

In the heart of a bustling city, Elen's life unfolded against the backdrop of a challenging childhood marked by parental disconnection. Her parents, Richard and Sarah, were emotionally distant, leaving Elen to navigate the turbulent seas of her emotions alone. Yet, amidst the emotional void, Elen discovered her refuge in music.

From a tender age, Elen's fingers danced effortlessly across piano keys, and her voice soared like a nightingale. Music became her secret language, a place where her unspoken emotions found expression. Despite the success she achieved as a talented musician, the echoes of her fractured past continued to reverberate through her life.

One evening, after a mesmerizing performance at a historic theater, Elen encountered a graceful elderly woman named Lillian. Lillian had once been a renowned musician in her own right, and her eyes twinkled with the wisdom of a life richly lived. She sensed the weight Elen carried in her heart.

Over cups of fragrant tea, Elen poured her heart out to Lillian. She spoke of her childhood, the disconnection with her parents, and the unquenchable thirst for emotional intimacy. Lillian, who had traversed her own trials, empathized deeply with Elen's longing for connection. Inspired by Lillian's wisdom and warmth, Elen made a brave decision to confront the shadows of her past. She embarked on a transformative journey of self-discovery and healing, seeking solace in the guidance of a compassionate therapist specializing in childhood emotional trauma.

In therapy, Elen navigated the labyrinth of her suppressed emotions, learning to embrace the pain she had long concealed. She realized that despite her adult success as a musician, the scars of her childhood lingered, like a haunting refrain in the background.

Elen's parents, observing their daughter's transformation, felt a profound awakening within themselves. They chose to join her in therapy, bravely acknowledging their emotional limitations and the impact on Elen's upbringing. It was a poignant reunion, as they began to grasp the depth of their daughter's pain.

As a family, they ventured into the heart of therapy, learning to communicate openly, practice empathy, and forge a haven of understanding. Elen's music, once a vessel for unspoken emotions, evolved into a medium of healing, as she composed melodies that narrated the story of her journey.

Elen's transformation unfolded like a melodious symphony. She discovered that while adult success was a notable achievement, it did not erase the profound effects of parental disconnection. However, with therapy and an unwavering commitment to healing, Elen found solace in the possibility of a future marked by emotional connection and reconciliation.

As she blossomed into adulthood, Elen carried the harmonious lessons from her journey. She understood that success was significant, but it could not supplant the yearning for emotional healing and connection borne of a challenging childhood. Elen's story resonated as an ode to resilience, a testament that even in the face of parental disconnection, one could compose their own melody of healing and hope, crafting a future of emotional harmony and unity.

CHAPTER 4

Ways to Recover and Heal After Being Raised by EI Parents

Despite being raised by an emotionally immature parent, this article shares five ways you can learn how to recover and heal after being raised by emotionally immature parents. Doing this allows you to recovery your true self – the person you always wanted to be – and cultivate healthier relationships in your life.

> "Humans share the primitive instinct that familiarity means safety" ~ John Bowlby

If we are raised in a chaotic home, we seek that out, even though we say and believe we want something different. If you grew up with emotionally immature parents, you might find yourself instinctively drawn to people who are emotionally unavailable, self-centered, and exploitive.

Despite the feelings of anger, loneliness, frustration, you feel there are ways you can heal and move on from being raised by emotionally immature parents. Taking these steps will help you grow and evolve as your own person, regardless of your first chapter - your family of origin and upbringing.

And making these changes for YOU, and no one else, will help you feel empowered and hopeful about your future both individually and collectively within a relationship.

Heal From Emotionally Immature Parents

Ways that include: giving up the current relationship you have with them, discovering and healing your fantasy, setting personal boundaries, understanding and clarifying your values, and engaging in self-care.

1. Let go of the fantasy.

It is common for children of emotionally immature parents to have the fantasy that their parent will change and begin to love them and show concern. As an adult you might continue to believe this and try different things in hopes of eliciting a response from your parent that will make you feel validated, heard, and loved.

And as an adult, you might have learned healthy communication skills and attempt to use these on your parent, to no avail.

Unfortunately, emotionally immature parents remain wedded to their own fantasy, expecting you - their child who is now an adult. - to continue to fix their childhood wounds and hurts.

The 'dance' that has been created between you and your parent continues until you decide to change the relational patterns that have been created.

Thus, the only way that things will change if you as the adult stop trying to convince your parent to change and be someone else, someone they are not capable of being for their own reasons.

Most adults continue to pursue the love, attention, and affection from their parent they never received in childhood and you may try to do that hoping that your parent will acknowledge how they hurt you, but they will not.

2. Take an observational approach.

Emotionally immature parents often create an enmeshed relationship with their child over individual identity. They don't respect boundaries and their are blurred lines between where they end and the child begins.

A person's true self is never acknowledged so you grow up not knowing who you really are, what you like, what you value, what you want out of life. Your decisions have been based on the enmeshed and unhealthy relationship you have with your parents.

Taking an observational approach means learning how to stay emotionally detached and how others are behaving in the world. Learn to think like a scientist. To recover from emotionally immature parents, try to ask yourself questions like:

- What am I noticing?
- How do they respond to I when you try to engage?
- What feelings are coming up?

If you start to get emotional, this means that your healing fantasy is being activated. You feel like unless they validate you (which they will not), you will be okay. If you are still in an emotional state, take a moment to step away, drink some water, splash some cold water on your face, - just create some distance - to help center yourself again.

Take the tiny baby steps you need to start creating space and healthier boundaries. This a very active approach to redefining the relationship and getting the emotional space you need to grow and recover.

3. Learn to express, then let go.

Sharing your feelings in a way that is calm and centered helps you gain mastery over your feelings without focusing on the outcome. They may or may not understand, empathize, or agree with you. That shouldn't be the focus. The goal should be, with any exchange, is healthy and clear communication, being able to recognize and articulate your thoughts and feelings, and feel good about the outcome.

This will help build your self-confidence and self-esteem and make you feel more in control of not only your feelings, but the situation and how you handled it.

When we are able to understand their emotional immaturity has more to do with them and less or nothing to do with you, you can begin to free yourself from the emotional loneliness you experienced.

Learning how to express how you feel to them, to yourself, or to others, allows you to return to yourself and begin to lead a more authentic life, free from the restrictions once put on you.

This allows you to free yourself from your frustration with them and eventually minimize your doubts you have about being lovable.

4. Focus on the outcome.

When people start to make changes on their end, they put expectations on the relationship and the person for it to go a certain way. Often, this is not how things play out. Ask yourself, what are you hoping to get from this exchange? Are you hoping they will change and understand you?
If so, maybe you should think about changing your goal because if it is focused on the other person, often we walk away feeling disappointed and frustrated.
So, maybe the goal should be more self focused. How do you want to show up in this exchange? What would healthy communication look like?

If you focus on the outcome and not the relationship, there is a greater likelihood that you feel better about the exchange rather than defeated.

Your parent will continue to behave as they do regardless of what you say or don't say. Thus the relationship will not change however, the outcome most likely will and this is where the growth and change takes place.

5. Create personal boundaries.

It is important to learn how to set healthy boundaries with your emotionally immature parent. However, when you begin to do this, they will do things that attempt to force you back into the enmeshed and unhealthy patterns. So, you must not take the bait.

Being able to identify the triggers that come up for you will help you identify when your parent is trying to 'suck you back into the unhealthy pattern.'

We all have triggers that affect us emotionally so creating a plan about how you will manage the triggers and come before you interact with your parent. Trying to figure it out in the moment, rarely if ever works.

Creating healthier boundaries means engaging in self-care. At the beginning, you may not know what self-care is or how you need because your life and all that you have been doing has been for your parent.

The focus has been on them, not you. You should expect that you wouldn't know where to start. Self-care means thinking about the things that bring you joy, how you want to spend your time, or even reading about self-care is and how you can start.

CHAPTER 4

How to Stop Emotionally Immature

Everyone gets annoyed with their parents from time to time. But if you have an emotionally immature parent, the struggles in your relationship run much deeper. If you do want to maintain a connection with your parents, it's important to be intentional with how you go about it. You can't change your parent, but you can change how you show up in the relationship.

Tips for how to handle emotionally immature parents

When I worked as a therapist, I met plenty of people with emotionally immature parents. Here are some of the strategies that actually helped them feel better about their relationships with their parents. Hopefully, they can help you, too.

1. Learn about emotionally immature parents

If you're reading this, there's a good chance that you're already well aware of what an emotionally immature parent is.

At the same time, there's always more to learn. And hearing from experts, as well as other people who've experienced the pain of emotionally immature parents, can really help in your healing process.

You could also look into other books, podcasts, and YouTube videos to learn more about emotionally immature parents and how to deal with them.

2. Let yourself feel your feelings

It sounds simple, but this is easier said than done for people with emotionally immature parents. You likely weren't taught the skills you need to identify, express, and embrace your emotions in a constructive way.

Thankfully, it's possible to learn these skills now. Depending on where you're at in your healing journey, you may be starting at square one—and that's okay.

Using this feelings wheel helped me when I first started my own journey in therapy. I've also given it to tons of clients who've used it to help themselves get more in touch with their own emotions. Start by checking in with yourself at least once a day and seeing which feelings on the wheel resonate with your current emotional state.

3. Be intentional about what you share

If you choose to continue a relationship with your parents, boundaries are key. You probably already know this in theory, but what does this actually look like in practice? Boundaries can take on tons of different forms, so let's start with something simple: what you choose to share with your parents.

Maybe you'd love to be able to go to your parent for emotional support around a difficult conversation with your boss. But if you know that past conversations about work have made you feel like s***, think twice before opening up. Let's be clear: I'm not advocating for relationships in which you have to hide parts of who you are. At the same time, it's also important to protect your energy if you still want to maintain a relationship with your parent(s).

4. Be as clear as possible about boundaries

Speaking of boundaries, it's important to be as clear as possible when setting boundaries with your emotionally immature parent.

For example, maybe your parent makes comments about your body that make you feel uncomfortable. In the past, you may have tried to brush these comments off or change the subject (which are valid responses, but may not be effective long-term).

If you're interested in setting a boundary, you could say something like: "It hurts my feelings when you make comments about my body. I don't want to talk about this with you, so if you continue saying these things, I'll end our phone call."

This outlines what exactly you need and expect from your parent so there's no ambiguity.

5. Enforce your boundaries

Communicating boundaries is only half the battle. They mean nothing if you don't follow through with them, and your relationship will stay the same if you don't enforce the boundaries you set.

To use the example above, this means actually hanging up the phone if your parent makes another comment about your body.

This might feel uncomfortable, harsh, or even mean if you're not used to enforcing your boundaries. It's okay if you feel this way, but don't let these emotions be an excuse to go back on your commitment to yourself.

Following through with your boundaries teaches your parents what you'll put up with and what you won't tolerate. Even if it doesn't change their actions in the long run, you'll build a sense of empowerment knowing that you have your own back.

6. Re-evaluate as needed

The boundaries you have with your parents right now don't need to be permanent. You can adjust them as your dynamic, needs, capacity, and emotional safety inevitably fluctuate.

Maybe you feel okay with having weekly phone calls with your parent right now. But if they keep making comments about your body, for example, it's within your control to cut down on the frequency.

If you notice that they respect your boundaries and you feel the desire to talk more often, you could consider chatting over FaceTime more frequently.

Of course, this is just an example to show that you're allowed to change your mind. Check in with yourself regularly to keep a pulse on what you need and how you're feeling.

7. Regulate before responding

If you notice feeling triggered by conversations with your parent (think: racing heart, feeling frozen, sweaty palms, feeling on edge, or having a tendency to snap back), learning how to regulate your emotions is key.

Texts and phone calls are a good place to start. When you see your parent's name pop up on your phone, take stock of what feelings come up. Consult your feelings wheel if needed

While it might be tempting to respond right away to get rid of any uncomfortable feelings you're having, I challenge you to take some space. You can return to the conversation once you feel more grounded.

The same goes for phone calls. You don't have to answer the phone if your parent calls you out of the blue. As for in-person conversations: it's always okay to ask for space or say that you need to think for a minute before responding to a question or request.

8. Adjust your expectations

Your parents may change their behavior over time—or they may not.

Adjusting your expectations is an important part of dealing with emotionally immature parents. It can be hard to let go of the hope that they'll go to therapy, take ownership of their behavior, prioritize your emotional needs over theirs, etc. It's okay to hope, but don't let that hope drive your decisions. Instead, focus on accepting the possibility (or reality) that your parent won't be able to show up for you in the way that you really want.

This realization can induce some intense feelings of grief, so be ready for that. It can also be helpful to adjust your expectations of yourself. For example, being the "perfect" child might not yield a different outcome in your relationship with your parent, so focus on showing up in a way you're proud of instead.

9. Get support

Navigating a relationship with an emotionally immature parent can be a grueling process full of heartache, anger, disappointment, and growing pains. But, it's also worth it for your mental and emotional well-being.

Getting support from other trusted sources is essential. Your other relationships can act as a refuge when you're in the thick of it. Can you share your feelings with your partner? Rely on a close friend to make you laugh and take your mind off of things? Consider the different ways you can connect with others.

I also recommend working with a therapist. While having people in your personal life who really get you is crucial, your therapist can give you specialized strategies and resources to help you process and heal.

Plus, your therapist can help you in a way that your loved ones can't. Since they're a third party who's not directly involved in your life, they can provide a unique, valuable perspective.

10. Remind yourself of your responsibilities

Being emotionally immature means that your parent's developmental age (in terms of their emotional development) doesn't necessarily match their chronological age. As a result, you may have had to "be the parent" in the relationship at times.

As a child, you didn't have a choice but to do this. You did what you needed to do in order to stay connected to your parent, which was essential for your survival.

Now that you're an adult, it's important to remind yourself what you're currently responsible for. While you may have been used to attending to your parent's emotional needs, you don't have to do that anymore.

Of course, it's one thing to know this logically and quite another to feel the truth of it in your heart. But reminding yourself of this can help ground yourself in the present and guide your decision when it comes to healing with your emotionally immature parent.

11. Be the parent that you need

On a similar note, now is your opportunity to be the parent you wish you had.

Let's circle back to the concept of grief. It can be incredibly painful to acknowledge that your parent wasn't and still isn't the parent you need them to be. Allow yourself to feel that grief.

While you can't go back in time and change your parent (or even change them in the present), you can tap into your inner parent. By letting yourself feel your feelings, setting boundaries, and having your own back, you're caring for yourself like a tender, loving parent.

If the whole "inner child" and "inner parent" thing doesn't resonate with you, consider thinking of the "big sister" or "big brother" version of yourself. You could also think of this as "higher self" if that language feels better for you.

12. Practice empathy

With all this talk of setting boundaries and remembering your responsibility to yourself, you might be wondering where empathy fits into the equation.

Let's tread lightly here. I'm not saying that you should condone your parent's behavior or explain it away by saying "they're doing the best they can" or "others have it worse." Instead, I see empathy as a way to avoid demonizing your parent and yourself. When healing from emotionally immature parents, you might feel tempted to blame your parent for all of your current problems. After all, if they were a better parent, you wouldn't be struggling in this way, right? That's true to some extent, but blaming is just a way of avoiding feelings. It doesn't actually solve anything or help you feel better in the long run. Instead, it creates a "versus mindset." (Not a technical term, but one that my partner came up with and my therapist has since adopted.)

If you view your relationship with your parent as a you vs. them situation, you're also banishing the parts of yourself that might struggle to put others' emotional needs first, push others' boundaries, or express yourself in a calm, constructive way.

All of this is to say that your conflict with your parent may also be reflective of an inner conflict of your own. By tapping into empathy for your parent's struggle, you can also find some grace for yourself.

13. Recognize that healing isn't an end-state

It's highly unlikely that you'll ever reach a place where you're done healing.

You might find that you're done trying to form a relationship with your parent (which is valid, by the way), but even this doesn't mean that your emotional processing stops.

Accepting that learning how to deal with an emotionally immature parent is an ongoing process can help manage your expectations and mitigate feelings of disappointment.

What to avoid when dealing with emotionally immature parents

We've discussed what you should try when navigating your relationship with an emotionally immature parent. Now, let's touch on some things to avoid.

- Don't backtrack on your boundaries. Like I said earlier, following through with your boundaries is key. A boundary without enforcement isn't a boundary.

- Don't match their energy. While it can be tempting to scream back at your parent or slam doors like they do, this won't help you heal in the long run.

- Don't feel guilty for taking care of yourself. Well, it's actually totally valid to feel guilty. Just honor this feeling without letting it derail your efforts to protect your emotional energy.

- Don't avoid it. It takes a lot of work to change your own patterns, and you might feel like it's easier to just keep going along with things the way they are. While this is certainly an option, you wouldn't be reading this if you weren't considering changing your approach.

- Don't be too hard on yourself. Dealing with an emotionally immature parent isn't easy, and you won't handle things perfectly every time. Be kind to yourself as you learn new ways to navigate your relationship.

Why learn how to deal with an emotionally immature parent

I've said more than once that dealing with immature parents isn't easy. If it was, you wouldn't be looking for tips
But the process is worth it, even if it ultimately doesn't change how your parent acts. Here's why.

- You'll become your #1. When you consistently set (and enforce) boundaries, you show yourself that you can have your own back. Support from others is necessary, but being able to truly rely on yourself is an irreplaceable feeling.

- You'll grow your own emotional maturity. All of the strategies I shared above are also ways to foster your own emotional growth. Emotional immaturity isn't a life sentence—you may not have been taught these skills, but you can learn them now.

- Your other relationships may benefit. Being intentional with how you approach your parent can also give you practice to make your other relationships even stronger, too.

- Your mental health can improve. Having an emotionally immature parent can take a toll on your overall well-being. These strategies can help you protect your emotional energy.

- You'll boost your self-esteem. Teaching your parent that you won't tolerate disrespectful (or downright abusive) behavior sends a message to yourself that you're worthy of respect. This can change how you treat yourself for the better.

CHAPTER 4

Lessons We Learned From Adult Children of EI Parents

On the outside, emotionally immature parents might look and act seemingly normal – they care for their child's physical health, provide meals, education, and a safe home. But, at the same time, they also tend to be uncomfortable with closeness and can fail to give their children the deep emotional connection they require.

1. The first step toward healing is to see your parents objectively

According to Gibson, most signs of emotional immaturity are beyond a person's conscious control and most emotionally immature parents have no awareness of how they've affected their children. That's why the goal of identifying your parent's traits and labeling their behavior is not to blame them, but to see them objectively, learn what to expect from them, and be less likely to get caught off guard by their limitations as a result.

The book underlines four main types of emotionally immature parents:

- **Emotional parents:** They have difficulty tolerating stress and emotional arousal, so they often lose their emotional balance and behavioral control in situations mature adults can handle. For example, they would treat small upsets like the end of the world. They are also prone to fluctuating moods and reactivity, which can make them unreliable and intimidating.

- **Driven parents:** They are compulsively goal-oriented and can't stop trying to perfect everything, including their children. Their emotional immaturity shows up in the way they make assumptions about other people, expecting everyone to want and value the same things they do. Rather than accepting their children's unique interests, they selectively praise and push what they want to see.

- **Passive parents:** They avoid dealing with anything upsetting and readily take a backseat to a dominant partner, even allowing abuse and neglect to occur by looking the other way. They cope by minimizing problems and acquiescing. Compared to the other types, these parents seem more emotionally available and can show some empathy for their children as long as the child fills the parent's need for an admiring, attentive companion.

- **Rejecting parents:** They usually don't want to spend time with their children and seem happiest when left alone. They struggle with emotional intimacy, their tolerance for other people's needs is practically nil, and their interactions consist of issuing commands, blowing up, or isolating themselves from family life.

It's important to note that the author states how each type exists along a continuum from mild to severe. Additionally, while most parents tend to fall into one category, many may be prone to behaviors that fit a different type when under certain kinds of stress.

2. By identifying your coping style, you might uncover the role you play

As claimed by Gibson, adult children with emotionally immature parents cope with emotional deprivation either by internalizing their problems or externalizing them. In other words, the first group believes it's up to them to change things, whereas the latter expects others to do it for them.

These coping mechanisms arise from parents inadequately responding to the child's true self. So, in order to connect with their parents, children develop a role-self to replace the spontaneous expression of their true self.

Gibson states that the process of assuming a role is unconscious and that it develops gradually, through trial and error, as children notice the reactions of their parents. As adults, these once-children tend to keep playing their roles in hopes that others will pay attention to them in the way they wished their parents had. This can be extremely tiring because it takes a huge effort to be something you are not, and it can negatively impact your overall wellbeing.

Here are some of the characteristics of the roles that adult children of emotionally immature parents play:

- Internalizers are self-reflective and often try to solve problems from the inside out and learn from their mistakes. They believe they can make things better by trying harder and instinctively take responsibility for solving problems independently. Their primary sources of anxiety are feeling guilty when they displease others and the fear of being exposed as imposters. They believe that the price of making a connection is to put other people first and treat them as more important, so they often think they can keep relationships by being the giver.

- Externalizers are reactive and do things impulsively to blow off anxiety quickly. For example, they would take action before they think things through. They are often not self-reflective and tend to assign blame to other people and circumstances rather than their own actions. They're firmly attached to the notion that things need to change in the outside world in order for them to be happy, believing that if only other people gave them what they want, their problems would be solved. Their main source of anxiety is that they will be cut off from the external sources their security depends upon, such as support from other people or financial success.

The author notes that which role is adopted is probably more a matter of personality and constitution than choice. As people move through life, they may go through periods of being more internalizing or externalizing, but their basic nature is likely to lean more one way than the other. In order to take the first move toward stepping away from these roles, Gibson suggests the following exercise:

1) Fold a piece of paper lengthwise down the middle, so you can only see one half of the page at a time, then write a heading on each half: "My True Self" and "My Role-Self".

2) Orient the paper so you only see the half with the heading "My True Self". Then think back to yourself as a child, before the age of eight, and answer the following questions:

- What was I interested in?
- Who were my favorite people, and what did I like about them?

- If I had free time, what did I like to do?
- How did I like to play? What was my idea of a perfect day?
- What really raised my energies?

3) Flip the paper over to the half with the heading "My Role-Self". Contemplate who you've had to become in order to feel admired and loved, and answer the following questions:

- Am I involved in things that I'm not interested in?
- What do I make myself do because you think it means I'm a good person?
- Are there people I'm involved with who deplete my energy and make me feel drained?
- How do I hope others see me?
- Which of my personality traits do I try to cover up?
- What am I glad nobody knows about me?

4) Put the piece of paper away for at least a day. Then open it up, smooth it down the middle, and compare the two sides.

The motive behind this exercise is to help you become more conscious of your true self. Once you decide to stop playing the role and live more from your true self, you might be able to pay attention to your genuine needs and desires.

3. There are two effective ways to handle emotionally immature parents

Adult Children of Emotionally Immature Parents offers two key approaches that can help you free yourself from getting caught up in your parent's emotional immaturity:

1) Detached observation: When interacting with emotionally immature parents, you'll feel more centered if you operate from a calm perspective rather than emotional reactivity. You can achieve this by:

- Practicing grounding exercises such as counting your breaths slowly or consciously relaxing one muscle at a time, starting with something simple, like your toes, and moving your way up through your body.
- Pretending you're conducting an anthropological field study and asking yourself what words you would use to describe your parents' facial expressions, what is their body language communicating, or does their voice sound calm or tense.
- Silently narrating your own emotional reactions because trying to find the exact words to describe something helps redirect your thoughts and avoid emotional reactivity.

2) Maturity awareness approach: This approach is about taking the emotional maturity of others into account and relating to them without getting upset. In order to achieve this, try:

- Expressing and then letting go: Try to say what you feel or want calmly and clearly without needing your parent to hear you or change. This way, you'll express your thoughts and have a sense of control without forcing them to empathize or understand.

- Focusing on the outcome, not the relationship: Try to reach a goal instead of going for empathy or understanding. For example, your clear goal could be something like, "I'll tell my parents I'm not coming home for Christmas," or "I'll ask my father to speak nicely to my children." This is achievable because you can ask others to listen, even though you can't make them understand.
- Managing, not engaging: Repeatedly redirect the conversation where you want it to go by gently easing their attempts to change the topic. At the same time, try to manage your emotions by observing and internally narrating your feelings rather than becoming reactive.

Healing from emotionally immature parents

After reading Adult Children of Emotionally Immature Parents, you might find relief from recognizing that you're not alone and that you're understood. You also might be able to spot signs of emotional immaturity and understand why you've often felt lonely.

That's a powerful first step toward healing.
However, while the skills from this book can be a valuable tool to sort through conflicting emotions, seeking help from a mental health professional can help you process your feelings of loss, hurt, and anger on a deeper level and help you bring understanding, patience, and compassion when it comes to interactions with your parents.

So don't hesitate to reach out to a professional and take another important step on your healing journey. Just because no one can do your inner work for you doesn't mean you can, should, or need to do it alone.

www.ingramcontent.com/pod-product-compliance
Lightning Source LLC
LaVergne TN
LVHW020050181025
823770LV00028B/634